TRADITIONS AND CELEBRATIONS

ST. PATRICK'S DAY

by Laura K. Murray

PEBBLE
a capstone imprint

Published by Pebble, an imprint of Capstone
1710 Roe Crest Drive, North Mankato, Minnesota 56003
capstonepub.com

Library of Congress Cataloging-in-Publication Data is available on the Library of Congress website.
ISBN: 9798875284533 (hardcover)
ISBN: 9798875284489 (paperback)
ISBN: 9798875284496 (ebook PDF)

Summary: Readers will discover the history of St. Patrick's Day as well as the many ways people around the world celebrate this Irish holiday.

Editorial Credits
Editor: Carrie Sheely; Designer: Heidi Thompson; Media Researcher: Rebekah Hubstenberger; Production Specialist: Tori Abraham

Image Credits
Dreamstime: Detry26, 25, Shelly Bychowski, 17; Getty Images: Archive Photos, 12, CEZARY ZAREBSKI PHOTOGRPAHY, 10, Charles McQuillan, 1, 5, 22, ilbusca, 11, iStock/Carlos Gonzalez Moyo, 14, iStock/Stephen Barnes, 9, Michael M. Santiago, 29, Peter Macdiarmid, 27, serkansenturk, 26, tarabird, 19, Theo Wargo, 13; Shutterstock: a katz, 28, Ballygally View Images, 7, Dalaifood, 20, Dennis MacDonald, 16, Eduard Moldoveanu, 15, Jon Osumi, cover, Pixel-Shot, 21, Renata Sedmakova, 6, Tatiana Gordievskaia, 23

Design Elements
Shutterstock: Rafal Kulik

Printed and bound in China. 006459

TABLE OF CONTENTS

Words in **bold** are in the glossary.

What Is St. Patrick's Day?

People line the streets to watch a big parade. Colorful floats and marching bands pass by. People dance as Irish music fills the air. Many people are dressed in green. Some have their faces painted. People wave Irish flags.

St. Patrick's Day is March 17. It began as a **religious** day. Today, it also celebrates Irish **culture**. Irish people show pride in their background. The holiday is nicknamed St. Paddy's Day. You don't need to be Irish to join the celebration!

St. Patrick is one of the world's most famous **saints**. He was born around the late 300s. Patrick wrote about his life. But there is a lot unknown.

A painting of St. Patrick in a church

St. Patrick is a **patron** saint of Ireland. But he wasn't born in Ireland. He was born in Roman Britain. Today, this area is England, Wales, and parts of Scotland.

As a teenager, Patrick was taken by Irish pirates. They brought him to Ireland. According to Patrick's writings, he was **enslaved** and made to work as a shepherd. He prayed to God for help.

St. Patrick is said to have been enslaved near Slemish Mountain in what is now Northern Ireland.

In his early 20s, Patrick got away. He sailed back home. He studied to be a **Catholic** priest. Later, he became a **bishop**. Patrick wanted people to learn about **Christianity**. This religion follows the teachings of Jesus Christ.

Patrick went back to Ireland to spread his message. Many people became Christian because of his teachings. They built churches. Patrick's work changed Ireland forever.

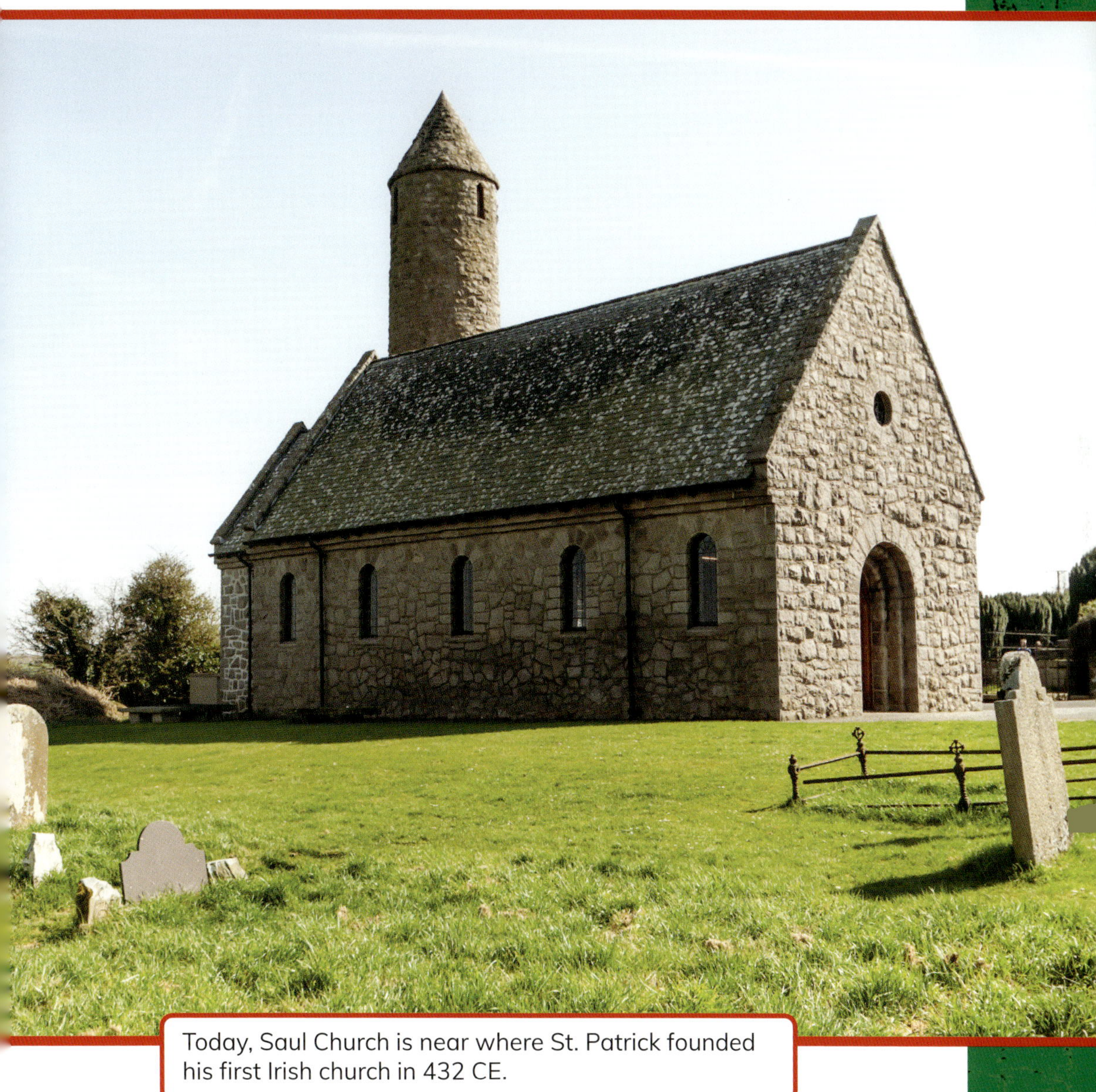

Today, Saul Church is near where St. Patrick founded his first Irish church in 432 CE.

Birth of a Holiday

One **legend** tells of St. Patrick and the shamrock. A shamrock is a green clover. It almost always has three leaves. St. Patrick used the shamrock in his teachings. It became a **symbol** of St. Patrick's Day.

St. Patrick (second from left) sometimes traveled with others to spread Christianity.

Another famous story is about St. Patrick and snakes. It says that he got rid of all the snakes in Ireland. But snakes have never lived in Ireland. The true meaning of the story remains unclear.

St. Patrick is often shown wearing a bishop headdress and holding a staff.

St. Patrick died on March 17. It may have been around the year 461. The Catholic Church made this day St. Patrick's Day.

Over the years, celebrating St. Patrick's Day spread. When people left Ireland, they brought their **traditions** with them. In the 1800s and 1900s, many Irish people moved to the United States. The **immigrants** celebrated their Irish background on St. Patrick's Day.

A St. Patrick's Day parade in New York City

Going Green

Green is everywhere on St. Patrick's Day! There are green clothes, decorations, lights, and food. Green is a symbol of Ireland. The country is known as the Emerald Isle. It has green hills and fields. Shamrocks are green. The Irish flag has green too.

Green, rolling hills near Ballintoy, Northern Ireland

The Empire State Building in New York City is lit for St. Patrick's Day.

Blue used to be the color of St. Patrick's Day. It was on ancient Irish flags and uniforms. But that changed in the late 1700s. The shamrock became an important symbol for Irish people. Green has been the Irish color ever since.

People wear green on St. Patrick's Day. You might get pinched if you don't! In Irish stories, leprechauns are a type of Irish fairy. They love playing tricks. They will pinch you. But they can't see people wearing green.

Even water turns green on St. Patrick's Day. The Chicago River flows through Illinois. Each year, boats spray dye into the river. The water turns bright green.

The dye in the Chicago River is only bright green for about three hours.

Time to Celebrate

The first St. Patrick's Day parade was held in 1601. It took place in what is now Florida. Today, many cities have parades on the holiday.

The sounds of marching bands and Irish music fill the air on St. Patrick's Day. People play fiddles, flutes, bagpipes, whistles, and more. There is Irish step dancing too. Dancers keep their upper bodies stiff. Their feet move fast! Many dancers wear traditional Irish costumes.

Playing bagpipes is an Irish musical tradition.

People enjoy traditional Irish food on St. Patrick's Day. They make potatoes, stew, shepherd's pie, and soda bread. People eat creamy mashed potatoes with cabbage. It is called colcannon. Corned beef and cabbage is a popular dish. It is not a common food in Ireland. But it was eaten by Irish immigrants.

Colcannon

Green foods help make St. Patrick's Day celebrations fun! Desserts are often decorated with green frosting or sprinkles. Dips, pastas, pancakes, and vegetables can be part of the green theme.

St. Patrick's Day celebrations can be very different from one another. People may have small gatherings with friends and family. A large celebration is held in Dublin, Ireland. It includes a national parade. A festival that includes plays and other performances lasts for several days.

Hundreds of people line the streets to watch the parade in Dublin, Ireland.

Rainbow crafts are popular on St. Patrick's Day. Rainbows stand for hope and luck.

Many schools have St. Patrick's Day parties. Children learn about Irish culture. They play games and make crafts. They enjoy tasty treats too!

People tell stories on St. Patrick's Day. In Irish stories, there are leprechauns and other fairies. The leprechauns are said to love gold.

Today, children in the United States make crafts called leprechaun traps. They decorate a box and set it out the night before St. Patrick's Day. The next day, children look for signs that a leprechaun visited. Coins or chocolate may be left behind.

People celebrate St. Patrick's Day in many parts of the world. It is a national holiday in Ireland. Australia, Canada, Great Britain, New Zealand, and the United States celebrate the day too. These countries have many people with Irish roots.

A St. Patrick's Day parade in Montreal, Canada

Catholics and others still honor the religious part of St. Patrick's Day. They may go to church services.

People celebrating St. Patrick's Day in London, England

St. Patrick's Day has a rich history. People remember the life of St. Patrick. Parades, parties, and decorations make it a fun day. But it is also a time to learn about Irish culture and traditions. Everyone is welcome to be part of the celebration!

GLOSSARY

bishop (BISH-op)—a high-ranking member of Christian leadership that is higher than a priest

Catholic (KATH-o-lik)—following the Christian religion of the Roman Catholic Church

Christianity (KRIS-chee-AN-eh-tee)—the belief in and following of the teachings of Jesus Christ

culture (KUHL-chur)—a group of people's beliefs, customs, and way of life

enslaved (en-SLAVED)—the practice of forcing people to do work with no pay

immigrant (IM-uh-gruhnt)—a person who leaves one country and settles in another

legend (LEDGE-end)—a traditional story that may not be true

patron (PAY-trun)—describes a chosen saint who is said to be a protector or helper for something, such as a country or type of job

religious (ree-LIJ-uhs)—having to do with a certain religion or one's spiritual beliefs

saint (SAYNT)—someone who is thought to be holy

tradition (truh-DISH-uhn)—a custom, idea, or belief passed down through time

READ MORE

Borgert-Spaniol, Megan. *Spring Crafts Across Cultures: 12 Projects to Celebrate the Season*. North Mankato, MN: Capstone, 2023.

Gibbons, Gail. *St. Patrick's Day*. New York: Holiday House, 2023.

Neuenfeldt, Elizabeth. *Throw a St. Patrick's Day Party*. Minneapolis: Bellwether Media, 2023.

INTERNET SITES

History.com: History of St. Patrick's Day
history.com/articles/history-of-st-patricks-day

National Geographic Kids: St. Patrick's Day
kids.nationalgeographic.com/celebrations/article/st-patricks-day

PBS: St. Patrick's Day: All About the Holidays
pbslearningmedia.org/resource/744f6cb7-4a1c-45d1-9f0a-98eb7b4bd6ed/st-patricks-day-all-about-the-holidays

INDEX

ABOUT THE AUTHOR

Laura K. Murray is the Minnesota-based author of more than 100 books for young readers. She loves helping others find their own story! Visit her at LauraKMurray.com.